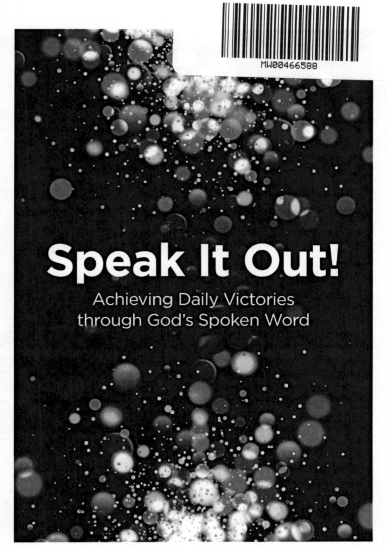

Speak It Out!

Achieving Daily Victories
through God's Spoken Word

Cheryl Delamarter

FIRST SILVER THREAD PUBLISHING EDITION, FEBRUARY 2018
Silver Thread Publishing is a division of A Silver Thread, Pismo Beach, CA
www.asilverthread.com
Copyright © 2017 by Cheryl Delamarter
Cover and Interior Design by Left Coast Design, Portland, OR
ISBN 978-09991794-5-1
Printed in the United States of America

Contents

Introduction	5
Daily with Jesus	7
Praise	9
Actions	12
Anger	14
Anxiety	16
Condemnation	18
Conformity	20
Courage	22
Defeat	24
Deliverance	26
Downcast	28
Excellence	30
Faith	32
Fear	34
Forgiven	36
Forgiving	38
Grace	40

Contents continued

Guidance   42

Humility   44

Jealousy   46

Love   48

Obedience   50

Peace   52

Peer Pressure   54

Pride   56

Purpose   58

Rejection   60

Strength   62

Thoughts   64

Victory   66

Wisdom   68

The Word   70

Be Empowered   72

Now It's Your Turn   73

Bibliography   78

Speak It Out!

Achieving Daily Victories through God's Spoken Word

Introduction

Let the word of Christ dwell in you richly in all wisdom; teaching and admonishing one another in psalms and hymns and spiritual songs, singing with grace in your heart to the Lord.

COLOSSIANS 3:16 KJV

Unhealthy emotions rob us of peace, joy, and contentment, ultimately leading to one's downfall. Generational sins, life experiences and circumstances cause us to develop strongholds that grip the heart and bring defeat. We must come against these challenges and face our battles daily with the power that brings victory. God's Spoken Word is our power, equipping us with the assurance and confidence to face life's challenges onto victory.

We live in a battle, not of flesh and blood, but against the rulers and authorities of this dark world and against the spiritual forces in the heavenly realm. (Ephesians 6:12) Our victory is in Jesus and in him alone, and the power we attain is through God's Spoken Word. As individuals learn to pray through the Scriptures, power, strength, and confidence will be theirs to fight and conquer unhealthy emotions that defeat and destroy. Learning the art of rejoicing and giving thanks IN all things, not FOR all things brings strength, knowing God Almighty will do a greater work through these circumstances. (1 Thessalonians 5:18) Equipped and empowered by God's Holy Word, individuals, young and old, will journey through life with victory, in the good times and the bad.

As the book's journey begins, each challenge is simply addressed, followed by a prayer and supportive Scripture verses, concluding with, "Speak It Out!" Prayers are designed to strengthen the heart, empower the spirit, and equip people of all ages to walk through life with God's Word at the forefront of their minds, being purposeful in applying it to everyday life. As we pray these prayers, learn and memorize portions of God's Word, we will be equipped to speak out, using the sword of the Spirit while facing daily challenges and defeating the enemy. (Ephesians 6:17) The more this is practiced, grateful hearts, faithful hearts, and purpose driven hearts will be the result of a life lived by the application of the Scriptures.

(Please note; the one-liners at the bottom of the pages are specifically designed to be short, yet powerful in speaking God's Word out loud to defeat the spiritual enemy. Unless quoted, they are paraphrased from the references given.)

This book is intended to supplement daily Bible reading, providing snippets of Scripture when the Bible is not at hand. Although the Bible verses noted on each page are taken from God's Word, it is of utmost importance to read the Bible in context to fully gain wisdom and discernment for daily life.

Daily Time with Jesus

Take time to quiet your heart, sit in the presence of the Lord, read His Word, pray, and don't forget to listen; listen for God's still voice. He wants to speak to your heart, refresh and strengthen you for the day, prepare the way, and direct your steps. Go ahead; open the Scriptures, open your heart, and let your Spirit be fed, your eyes enlightened from the Words of God the Father, Jesus the Son, allowing the Holy Spirit to move you!

Jesus answered, "It is written: 'Man does not live on bread alone, but on every word that comes from the mouth of God.'
MATTHEW 4:4 NIV

Pray

Open my eyes
That I may behold
Wondrous things
Out of thy law, O Lord (Psalm 119:18)

Thank you, dear Jesus,
Amen

When you rise

In the morning, O Lord, you hear my voice; in the morning I lay my requests before you and wait in expectation.

PSALM 5:3-4 NIV

Satisfy us in the morning with your unfailing love, that we may sing for joy and be glad all our days!

PSALM 90:14 NIV

When you lie down to sleep:

I will lie down and sleep in peace, for you alone, O Lord, make me dwell in safety.

PSALM 4:8 NIV

As you journey through the day and night, let your mouths be filled with praise!

My mouth is filled with your praise, declaring your splendor all day long.

PSALM 71:8 NIV

Praise and worship is God's language. It precedes all other prayers, driving away the negative thoughts and feelings that can lead to defeat. As we develop hearts of praise, our daily walk will be filled with peace and joyful expectation!

Because thy loving kindness is better than life, my lips shall praise thee. Thus will I bless thee while I live: I will lift up my hands in thy name. My soul shall be satisfied as with marrow and fatness; and my mouth shall praise thee with joyful lips: When I remember thee upon my bed, and meditate on thee in the night watches.

PSALM 63:3-6 KJV

Let the Journey Begin!

As we begin our journey choosing to confront daily battles through the Scriptures, let us start by developing a heart of praise! Praise honors God and keeps our hearts centered on him.

PRAISE!

Once a heart is surrendered to Jesus, lips that praise Him reap a harvest of joy. Praise keeps our focus on the One who saves us, releases God's power to ward off the enemy, resulting in hearts overflowing with thankfulness for God's goodness and faithfulness in our lives. Praise is at the heart of all that is good, flooding the soul with happiness; that joy may abound!

Start and end each day with praise and all the hours in between. Your prayers throughout the day need not be lengthy; phrases or words of praise works!

"Praise Jesus!"
"You are my God, my heart praises you!"
"Praise Jesus who redeems my life and fills my heart with joy!"

Our words of praise not only bless the heart of God, they cultivate a joyful heart within us as well. Let us develop a heart of praise and thanksgiving by being purposeful in praising our Lord daily, not only for all his blessings, but for who he is, Lord and Savior, Jesus, King of kings!

🙏 PRAY!

"Because your love is better than life," (Psalm 63:3a NIV)
I will praise you with my whole heart, O Lord!
I praise my Savior and my God
My redeemer, my Lord!

How I praise your Holy Name!
My life is in your hands
Praise be to Jesus!

Amen

🅰 FROM GOD'S WORD

It is a good thing to give thanks unto the Lord, and to sing praises unto thy name, O most High: To shew forth thy loving-kindness in the morning, and thy faithfulness every night,

PSALM 92:1-2 KJV

I will praise the name of God with a song; I will magnify him with thanksgiving. This will please the Lord more than an ox or a bull with horns and hoofs.

PSALM 69:30-31 RSV
(Praise is more pleasing to God than sacrifice!)

But as for me, I will always have hope; I will praise you more and more. My mouth will tell of your righteousness, of your salvation all day long, though I know not its measure.

PSALM 71:14-15 NIV

💬 SPEAK IT OUT!

Praise the Lord, O my soul, all that is within me praise his Holy Name; who forgives my sins, heals my diseases, and redeems my life from the pit! Praise his Holy Name! (Psalm 103:1-4a)

Additional Verses from Your Scripture Reading

SPEAK IT OUT!

NOTE

The following pages are titled with a word or phrase for which prayer is needed. They are arranged alphabetically, each reflecting a concern or need. Prayers are scripted for you. The words at the bottom of the pages are mostly paraphrased from portions of Scripture, to speak out loud bringing victory through the power of God's Spoken Word. The verses beside portions of the prayers and at the end of the "Speak It Out" section, provide reference to the Scriptures. May you experience power, strength, and victory as you pray through God's Word!

ACTIONS

Actions speak volumes, louder than words. People are watching when we least expect. Let us be diligent to think before we act. Become aware of how our actions will affect others keeping in mind, as children of King Jesus, we are to do our best to reflect him in all circumstances. As it says in Isaiah 61:3b, we are called "oaks of righteousness for the display of his splendor."

Get in the habit of asking, "Are my actions displaying the splendor of my Lord and Savior, Jesus Christ?" Think, act, and respond accordingly.

PRAY!

O Lord,

I'm not proud of my actions lately
I am short tempered, my words unkind
Please forgive me
Help me to act in the way that pleases you
Teach me to treat others with kindness
And remember to treat others as I wish to be treated

Let my words, my actions,
The meditations of my heart
Be pleasing to you, O Lord,
My Rock and my Redeemer (Psalm 19:14)

In Jesus name,
Amen

✝ FROM GOD'S WORD

So in everything, do to others what you would have them do to you, for this sums up the Law and the Prophets.

MATTHEW 7:12 NIV

Do nothing out of selfish ambition or vain conceit, but in humility consider others better than yourselves.

PHILIPPIANS 2:3 NIV

And let us consider how we may spur one another on toward love and good deeds.

HEBREWS 10:24 NIV

💬 SPEAK IT OUT!

I am a child of King Jesus brought into the world for the display of his splendor! I choose to act accordingly!

Additional Verses from Your Scripture Reading

ANGER

Anger can be deadly! It results in careless, hurtful speech and destructive actions causing deep wounds. We are to be slow to anger and abounding in love as the Lord is to us! (Psalm 86:15, 103:8) There are moments we might need to exercise righteous anger in response to disrespect, irreverence and the like. This kind of anger, however, should result in positive actions toward a positive outcome.

Anger should not go unchecked. Only a fool gives full vent to his anger. (Proverbs 29:11) Let us not be fools; instead let us be self-controlled, our words and actions glorifying our Lord.

 PRAY!

Dear Lord,

I am easily angered which is not pleasing to you
Forgive me for my unleashed anger
Help me to be self-controlled with a heart of love
Responding to others with care and respect

If I have reason to be angry
Give me strength and wisdom to respond in a way
That glorifies you, resulting in a positive outcome
I praise you for delivering me from my sinful anger!

In Jesus name,
Amen

✝ FROM GOD'S WORD

A fool gives full vent to his anger, but a wise man keeps himself under control.

PROVERBS 29:11 NIV

"In your anger do not sin." Do not let the sun go down while you are still angry, and do not give the devil a foothold.

EPHESIANS 4:26-27 NIV

Know this, my beloved brethren. Let every man be quick to hear, slow to speak, slow to anger, for the anger of man does not work the righteousness of God.

JAMES 1:19-20 RSV

💬 SPEAK IT OUT!

Anger does not bring about the righteousness God has for me! (James 1:21) Deliver me from anger, Lord Jesus!

Additional Verses from Your Scripture Reading

ANXIETY

Anxiety cripples, defeats, bringing irrational thoughts to our minds, and at times fear to our hearts. It keeps us from thriving in daily life. The cure for anxiety is trust. If we trust the Lord with ALL of our hearts (Proverbs 3:5a) and not fret in our limited human understanding, we are free to be and live moment by moment in peace.

 PRAY!

Oh Lord,

I am feeling anxious, nervous
My mind is busy, unsettled
Help me to focus on you

In obedience,
I cast my anxiety on you
So that your peace
Which goes beyond all understanding
Will guard my heart and mind in Christ Jesus (Philippians 4:7)

Praise Jesus!
My victory is in You!
Amen

✝ FROM GOD'S WORD

Have no anxiety about anything, but in everything by prayer and supplication with thanksgiving let your requests be made known to God. And the peace of God, which passes all understanding, will keep your hearts and your minds in Christ Jesus.

PHILIPPIANS 4:6-7 RSV

Cast all you anxieties on him, for he cares about you.

I PETER 5:7 RSV

Trust in the Lord with all thine heart; and lean not unto thine own understanding. In all thy ways acknowledge him, and he shall direct thy paths.

PROVERBS 3:5-6 KJV

💬 SPEAK IT OUT!

I will not be anxious, but thankful, Lord, for my trust is in you! Your peace guards my heart and mind in Christ Jesus. (Philippians 4:6-7)

Additional Verses from Your Scripture Reading

CONDEMNATION

Jesus Christ and his grace offer us freedom from condemnation, sin, and death. When we sin and are truly sorry, Jesus forgives and cleanses, purifying us from sin's ugliness and destruction. Satan works to fester guilt and condemnation in our hearts. His plan is to draw us away from God and bring defeat! We need to cling to God, for he wants to bring healing and restoration.

Confess your sins; keep your heart right with Jesus, and be blessed! This keeps our line of communication open with him; our hearts pure and moldable to become all God would have us to be.

PRAY

Jesus,

I am ever so thankful that you know my every thought,
My every action
When the lies of the enemy try to touch my heart
To condemn me
I know YOU are greater than my heart (1 John 3:20)
I am in Christ Jesus!
There is no condemnation to those who are in Christ Jesus
Therefore, I am NOT condemned!

How I praise your Holy Name, Jesus!
Amen

✝ FROM GOD'S WORD

There is therefore now no condemnation to them which are in Christ Jesus, who walk not after the flesh, but after the Spirit. For the law of the Spirit of life in Christ Jesus hath made me free from the law of sin and death.

ROMANS 8:1-2 KJV

This then is how we know that we belong to the truth, and how we set our hearts at rest in his presence whenever our hearts condemn us. For God is greater than our hearts, and he knows everything.

1 JOHN 3:19-20 NIV

Nay, in all these things we are more than conquerors through him that loved us. For I am persuaded, that neither death, nor life, nor angels, nor principalities, nor powers, nor things present, nor things to come, nor height, nor depth, nor any other creature, shall be able to separate us from the love of God, which is in Christ Jesus our Lord.

ROMANS 8:37-39 KJV

💬 SPEAK IT OUT!

I am in Christ Jesus, therefore in NO WAY am I condemned; I am set free from sin and death! Praise to my Savior and Lord, Jesus Christ! (From Romans 8:1)

Additional Verses from Your Scripture Reading

CONFORMITY

You, child of God, are to be set apart! Although living in this world, we are not of this world. Do not allow yourself to be conformed to the culture that is ever-changing. Be transformed daily by the renewing of your minds according to God's Holy Word. Be strong, have the courage to be different, and allow the Lord to use your unique giftedness to make a difference in the world we live in.

You were created in God's image. Keep your relationship with Jesus intimate, so he can speak to your heart and transform you into his likeness. Our kingdom is the eternal kingdom. Do not settle for the ways of the world. Live to bring others to Jesus and into His eternal kingdom, where pain and sorry cease; joy abounds!

PRAY!

Dear Lord Jesus,

By your Spirit living within me
I will not be conformed to this world
But be transformed by the renewing of my mind (Romans 12:2)
According to your Holy Word

Help me to be strong and courageous
Resist the lies of the enemy
Flee from evil, clinging to all that is good!

Oh, that I should live to reflect your goodness,
Your glory, and your truth!
Loving you always and forever,
Amen

✝ FROM GOD'S WORD

If we live, we live to the Lord; and if we die, we die to the Lord. So, whether we live or die, we belong to the Lord.

ROMANS 14:8 NIV

And be not conformed to this world: but be ye transformed by the renewing of your mind, that ye may prove what is that good, and acceptable, and perfect, will of God.

ROMANS 12:2 KJV

For those who live according to the flesh set their minds on the things of the flesh, but those who live according to the Spirit set their minds on the things of the Spirit. To set the mind on the flesh is death, but to set the mind on the Spirit is life and peace.

ROMANS 8:5-6 RSV

💬 SPEAK IT OUT!

I will not be conformed to this world, but transformed by the renewing of my mind through Christ Jesus! (Romans 12:2)

Additional Verses from Your Scripture Reading

COURAGE

Oftentimes, we need courage to face the moment, try a new task, confront, perform, present to a group. We need courage to do what is right and good, courage to become the men and women God desires for us to be. Our Lord empowers his children to be strong and courageous! Journey through life with him, in his strength, trusting Jesus to go before us to bring victory!

 PRAY!

Lord Jesus,

I need courage today
I feel timid and nervous, yet
Greater is he in me
Than he that is in the world! (I John 4:4)

I move forward with confidence, strength, and courage
Knowing you, Father God,
Go before me with victory
Praise Jesus!

My victory is in You!
Amen

🔲 FROM GOD'S WORD

Be on your guard; stand firm in the faith; be men of courage; be strong.

1 CORINTHIANS 16:13A NIV

Be strong and courageous. Do be afraid or terrified because of them, for the Lord your God goes with you; he will never leave you nor forsake you.

DEUTERONOMY 31:6 NIV

Ye are of God, little children, and have overcome them: because greater is he that is in you, than he that is in the world.

1 JOHN 4:4 KJV

💬 SPEAK IT OUT!

I am strong and courageous, for greater is he who is in me than he that is in the world! Praise your Holy Name, Jesus! (Deuteronomy 31:6, 1 John 4:4)

Additional Verses from Your Scripture Reading

DEFEAT

How easy it is to allow our feelings to defeat us; yet, nothing good comes from it. Let us not give into the emotional turmoil that grips our hearts, spiraling us downward to defeat.

Recognize Satan's plan is to defeat and destroy, ultimately hindering us from moving forward in God's purpose. We must fight a defeated spirit through the power of prayer, with hope and confidence in our God who is for us, not against us! (Romans 8:31b) Acknowledge and embrace the promises of God through his Word, for we are more than conquerors through Christ who loves us! (Romans 8:37)

 PRAY!

O Lord Jesus,

I feel defeated
This is not of you!
Breathe your life into me
That I may live this day
With passion and purpose
Joy and expectation
Life to the full!

For your glory, dear Jesus!
In your name, I pray,
Amen

✝ **FROM GOD'S WORD**

What shall we then say to these things? If God be for us, who can be against us?

ROMANS 8:31 KJV

The thief comes only to steal and kill and destroy; I have come that they may have life, and have it to the full.

JOHN 10:10 NIV

No, in all these things we are more than conquerors through him who loved us.

ROMANS 8:37 NIV

💬 **SPEAK IT OUT!**

Jesus came that I might have abundant life! (John 10:10)
Breathe life into me, Lord Jesus!

Additional Verses from Your Scripture Reading

DELIVERANCE

In this fallen world, we carry around so much "stuff" in our minds and hearts that weigh us down. These thoughts and feelings chip away at our worth, our values bringing defeat, eventually robbing us of joy and contentment. Sinful desires, generational strongholds, bondage, the burdens of life, the weight of sin keep us from flourishing as Jesus would have us to.

Jesus came to deliver us from sin and death! (Romans 8:2) He came to set the captive free! (Isaiah 61:1). We need to recognize the things that bind us, preventing the beauty of Christ's love to shine through; and pray for deliverance in the name of Jesus! Be delivered; be set free!

🙏 PRAY

Dear Lord,

You came to set the captive free! (Isaiah 61:1)
Deliver me from all that binds me,

_____ *(Name them)*

From any darkness that threatens me

I walk in the light of Christ Jesus
Who has set me free from sin and death (Romans 8:2)
With your strength and courage
I will stand firm and be still

For I know that you are God!
My deliverance comes from you!
Praise Jesus!
Amen

📕 FROM GOD'S WORD

From the Lord comes deliverance. May your blessing be on your people.

PSALM 3:8 NIV

And the Lord shall help them, and deliver them: he shall deliver them from the wicked, and save them, because they trust in him.

PSALM 37:40 KJV

The Lord is my rock, and my fortress, and my deliverer, my God, my rock, in whom I take refuge, my shield, and the horn of my salvation, my stronghold. I call upon the Lord, who is worthy to be praised, and I am saved from my enemies.

PSALM 18:2-3 RSV

The righteous cry, and the LORD heareth, and delivereth them out of all their troubles.

PSALMS 34:17 (KJV)

💬 SPEAK IT OUT!

Lord, my rock in whom I take refuge, I know you hear my cry; deliver me from _____! *(Name your need for deliverance)* (Psalm 18:2, Psalms 34:17)

Additional Verses from Your Scripture Reading

DOWNCAST

We live amidst challenges, disappointments and heartaches, oftentimes resulting in a downcast and disheartened spirit. Satan, especially during these times, tempts us toward hopelessness.

God desires to strengthen and refine us through our trials. He will use them to develop us into stronger men and women of character, leading us to a brighter tomorrow! Never lose hope, for God is working on our behalf and will work all things for our good, as long as we continue with him. (See Romans 8:28) Trust Him!

 PRAY

Dear Lord,

My heart is sad
My spirit, disturbed
Yet, my hope is in you
I praise you, my Savior, and my God!

Satan has no power over me
I receive the Lord's deliverance and rejoice
For he alone has set me free!
My heart will sing for joy!

Praise the Lord, O my soul
ALL that is within me praise his Holy Name! (Psalm 103:1)
Amen, Dear Jesus,
Amen

🕀 FROM GOD'S WORD:

Why are you downcast, O my soul?
Why so disturbed within me?
Put your hope in God, for I will yet praise him,
My Savior and my God.

PSALM 42:11 NIV

… he hath sent me to bind up the brokenhearted, to proclaim liberty
to the captives, and the opening of the prison to them that are bound;
ISAIAH 61:1B KJV

… to give unto them beauty for ashes, the oil of joy for mourning, the
garment of praise for the spirit of heaviness;
ISAIAH 61:3A KJV

💬 SPEAK IT OUT!

The Lord is my lamp; he turns my darkness into light!
(2 Samuel 22:29) I receive your light; praise Jesus!

Additional Verses from Your Scripture Reading

EXCELLENCE

You, fellow believer, are a child of The King! It is of utmost importance to live a life of excellence, reflecting the beauty of our Savior. God has a plan and a purpose for each of his children. Our duty is to strive to be our best in all things. Christ then can work out his best for our lives and accomplish the purpose he has for us presently and into his eternal kingdom!

 PRAY!

Dear Lord,

I want to be a child of excellence
Help me to work with diligence
Persevering with my whole heart
Always as unto you, Lord! (Colossians 3:23)

Thank you for helping me to be my best
So you can do your best through me
For my good
For your glory, Jesus!

Amen

✝ FROM GOD'S WORD

And whatever you do, in word or deed, do everything in the name of the Lord Jesus, giving thanks to God the Father through him.

COLOSSIANS 3:17 RSV

Whatever your task, work heartily, as serving the Lord and not men, knowing that from the Lord you will receive the inheritance as your reward; you are serving the Lord Christ.

COLOSSIANS 3:23-24 RSV

Don't let anyone look down on you because you are young, but set an example for the believers in speech, in life, in love, in faith and in purity.

I TIMOTHY 4:12 NIV

Therefore, my dear brothers, stand firm. Let nothing move you. Always give yourselves fully to the work of the Lord, because you know that your labor in the Lord is not in vain.

I CORINTHIANS 15:58 NIV

💬 SPEAK IT OUT!

I will do all things with all of my heart as unto the Lord! (Colossians 3:23)

Additional Verses from Your Scripture Reading

FAITH

Our faith is a shield that protects our minds, our hearts, and our actions. It is a weapon used to stand against the evil one and live victoriously. Believing in Jesus Christ, knowing and trusting his attributes and his Word, not wavering according to the truth and promises of the Scriptures, strengthens our faith. Read the Bible daily, pray with thanksgiving, and cling to God's promises. Let your faith be strong and unending!

 PRAY!

Strengthen my shield of faith, O Lord!
I will not doubt
For you, the Creator of the heavens and the earth,
Love me with an incomprehensible love!

Help me, Lord,
To know you better
Love you deeper
Live life with unwavering faith!

Praise the Name of Jesus!
Amen

✝ FROM GOD'S WORD

If you do not stand firm in your faith, you will not stand at all.

ISAIAH 7:9b NIV

So then, just as you received Christ Jesus as Lord, continue to live in him, rooted and built up in him, strengthened in the faith as you were taught, and overflowing with thankfulness.

COLOSSIANS 2:6 NIV

But without faith it is impossible to please him: for he that cometh to God must believe that he is, and that he is a rewarder of them that diligently seek him.

HEBREWS 11:6 KJV

Above all, taking the shield of faith, wherewith ye shall be able to quench all the fiery darts of the wicked.

EPHESIANS 6:16 KJV

💬 SPEAK IT OUT!

My faith is in you, O Lord, my rock and my redeemer in whom I trust! I will not waver!

Additional Verses from Your Scripture Reading

FEAR

There are times we have reason to be afraid, but more often than not, our fears are unsupported. We fear the unknown, failure, people's disapproval, the future. Whatever the reason (outside of a healthy, reverent fear of the Lord), fear is not of the Lord. In fact, there are numerous verses in the Scriptures stating specifically not to be fearful or be afraid. A life surrendered to Jesus Christ has the Holy Spirit. Through the power of Christ within, we are able to come against any fear with victory.

🙏 PRAY!

I lift up my hands and my head to you, O Lord,
Proclaiming, "I will not be afraid!"
For God has not given me the spirit of fear,
But of power, of love and a sound mind! (2Timothy 1:7)

Thank you, Dear Jesus,
Amen!

The following Scripture can be a prayer in itself. The verse below would be one to memorize and speak out loud when feeling nervous or anxious of what others may think of us or of our performance.

"When I am afraid, I will trust in you.
In God, whose word I praise,
In God I trust; I will not be afraid.
What can mortal man do to me?"
Psalm 56:3-4 NIV

✝ FROM GOD'S WORD

Fear not, for I am with you, be not dismayed, for I am your God; I will strengthen you, I will help you, I will uphold you with my victorious right hand.

ISAIAH 41:10 RSV

For God hath not given us the spirit of fear; but of power, and of love, and of a sound mind.

2 TIMOTHY 1:7 KJV

I sought the Lord, and he heard me, and delivered me from all my fears.

PSALM 34:4 KJV

💬 SPEAK IT OUT!

I will not be afraid; for God does not give me the spirit of fear, but of power, love, and a sound mind! (2 Timothy 1:7)

Additional Verses from Your Scripture Reading

FORGIVEN

When feeling remorse for a sin committed, confess to Jesus. He is faithful and just to forgive and cleanse us from all unrighteousness! (1 John 1:9) As humans, it is difficult to fully grasp the beauty and completeness of grace. We feel the need to do something to earn forgiveness. Through Christ Jesus, it is finished; he alone paid the price! All we need to do is confess our sins and receive the gift of forgiveness.

Satan wants us to live in guilt and condemnation. With those feelings oppressing us, pray through the Scriptures that promise forgiveness, cleansing us from all unrighteousness. Do not allow condemnation to defeat and destroy. Jesus turns our scarlet sins white as snow (Isaiah 1:18), purifying us to live for his glory into his eternal kingdom.

🙏 PRAY!

I am so sorry, Jesus, for I have sinned against you
Please forgive me for _____ *(State the sin)*
Help me to be strong
Never to repeat this sin again!

Strengthen me to live right before you
You took the punishment for my sin
Sins once as scarlet
By your forgiveness, are now white as snow. (Isaiah 1:18)

Through Jesus Christ, I am forgiven
I stand in awe of my Savior
I bow before you with a forgiven, grateful heart
Praising your holy name!

Amen

✝ FROM GOD'S WORD

In him we have redemption through his blood, the forgiveness of sins, in accordance with the riches of God's grace that he lavished on us with all wisdom and understanding.

EPHESIANS 1:7-8 NIV

If we confess our sins, he is faithful and just to forgive us our sins, and to cleanse us from all unrighteousness.

I JOHN 1:9 KJV

When we were overwhelmed by sins, you forgave our transgressions.

PSALM 65:3 NIV

💬 SPEAK IT OUT!

Jesus, because of you, I am a forgiven child of God, pure in your sight; praise your Holy Name!

Additional Verses from Your Scripture Reading

FORGIVING

When we are wronged, we often feel justified in not forgiving; yet Jesus says we are to forgive as he has forgiven us. There is absolutely no comparison of our sins against Father God to the sins others have afflicted upon us. No matter how terribly offensive another sins against us, we need to choose to forgive, whether or not they ask and whether or not it is deserved.

This is a choice we make in obedience to what God requires of us. Our forgiveness does not justify the offender; instead, it frees us from the bondage that results from an unforgiving heart. How beautiful is that?

🙏 PRAY!

O Lord,

I choose to forgive _____ for _____.
My heart does not feel forgiving
But I choose to forgive
For you command us to forgive one another
As you have forgiven us!

Heal my brokenness
Help me to never forget the touch of your forgiveness
So I too will forgive
As I forgive, you will forgive me
Setting me free to live in wholeness and in love

Thank you, Jesus,
Amen

✝ FROM GOD'S WORD

For if ye forgive men their trespasses, your heavenly Father will also forgive you: But if ye forgive not men their trespasses, neither will your Father forgive your trespasses.

MATTHEW 6:14-15 KJV

Bear with each other and forgive whatever grievances you may have against one another. Forgive as the Lord forgave you. And over all these virtues put on love, which binds them all together in prefect unity.

COLOSSIANS 3:13-14 NIV

(Learn to love the unlovely, forgive the offender).

Be kind and compassionate to one another, forgiving each other, just as in Christ God forgave you.

EPHESIANS 4:32 NIV

💬 SPEAK IT OUT!

In obedience to Jesus, I forgive _____!

(State who you forgive and for what they did against you)

Additional Verses from Your Scripture Reading

GRACE

Grace, God's beautiful grace is a gift freely given to all. With opened arms and surrendered hearts, we receive this incomprehensible gift! The abundant life here and now, life forever is all about God's marvelous grace. By the grace of Jesus Christ, we can live a life delivered from the slimy pit of sinfulness (leading to destruction and spiritual death) to a life redeemed for holiness, purity, and truth.

 PRAY!

O Lord,

I am in awe and humbled by your grace
Saving me from sin and death!
With opened arms and a surrendered heart
I receive your incomprehensible gift of grace

Oh, that I should live daily
Moment by moment
All the years of my life
In humble adoration of your amazing grace

Praise the name of Jesus
Who did it all, for me!
Amen

🔲 FROM GOD'S WORD

For all have sinned, and come short of the glory of God; Being justified freely by his grace through the redemption that is in Christ Jesus:

ROMANS 3:23-24 KJV

But because of his great love for us, God, who is rich in mercy, made us alive with Christ even when we were dead in transgressions – it is by grace you have been saved.

EPHESIANS 2:4-5 NIV

For by grace you have been saved through faith; and this is not your own doing, it is the gift of God – not because of works, lest any man should boast.

EPHESIANS 2:8-9 RSV

That being justified by his grace, we should be made heirs according to the hope of eternal life.

TITUS 3:7 KJV
(See also verses 4-7)

💬 SPEAK IT OUT!

I am a sinner saved by your redeeming grace, alive with Christ; praise the Holy Name of Jesus! (Ephesians 2:5)

Additional Verses from Your Scripture Reading

GUIDANCE

Every day we make decisions; small decisions, big decisions, decisions that guide the course of our lives. God knows our every step and our hope is to walk in step with him. It is our responsibility to follow him, spend time daily in his Word, and with Jesus in prayer.

As this becomes a daily habit, a lifestyle, God transforms the heart leading and guiding our decisions. Since the good Lord knows what is best for us, if we take time to know him, he will naturally be our guide. As we develop an intimate relationship with Jesus, his desires become ours, and the Holy Spirit within us guides and directs our steps.

🦵 PRAY!

Dear Jesus,

Your Word is a lamp to my feet,
A light for my path (Psalm 119:105)
Give me an undivided heart
To walk with you always!

You know the path I am to take
Show me your way, O Lord
I trust you to direct my steps
For my journey is secure in you

Thank you, Dear Jesus,
Amen

🕇 FROM GOD'S WORD

Teach me thy way, O Lord; I will walk in thy truth: unite my heart to fear thy name.

PSALM 86:11 KJV

Commit thy works unto the Lord, and thy thoughts shall be established.
PROVERBS 16:3 KJV

In his heart a man plans his course, but the Lord determines his steps.
PROVERBS 16:9 NIV

I will praise the Lord, who counsels me; even at night my heart instructs me. I have set the Lord always before me. Because he is at my right hand, I will not be shaken.

PSALM 16:7-8 NIV

💬 SPEAK IT OUT!

I commit my plans to you, O Lord, trusting you to direct my steps! (Proverbs 16:3, 9)

Additional Verses from Your Scripture Reading

HUMILITY

A humble heart is a blessed heart! Let our focus be Christ-centered, other-centered, rather than self-centered. We are God's creation; he has gifted his children with talents and abilities for a specific purpose to glorify him. We must work to develop ourselves to become the best we can be, with full knowledge that our gracious God is the giver of every perfect gift. (James 1:17) Let us remain humble before the Lord, that he may lift us up! (James 4:10)

 PRAY!

O Lord,

How I long to remain humble before you
Honoring others above myself (Romans 10:12)
I pray my thoughts, words, and actions
Glorify you, that others may see Jesus in me

Thank you for the gifts and talents you've given me
Use me, Lord, as your vessel
For your purpose, for your glory
Praise your Holy Name, Jesus!

Amen

✝ FROM GOD'S WORD

Humble yourselves in the sight of the Lord, and he shall lift you up.

JAMES 4:10 KJV

For whoever exalts himself will be humbled, and whoever humbles himself will be exalted.

MATTHEW 23:12 NIV

Do nothing from selfishness or conceit, but in humility count others better than yourselves. Let each of you look not only to his own interests, but also to the interests of others.

PHILIPPIANS 2:3-4 RSV

Be devoted to one another in brotherly love. Honor one another above yourselves.

ROMANS 12:10 NIV

💬 SPEAK IT OUT!

Keep my heart humble, O Lord; I want my life to glorify you!

Additional Verses from Your Scripture Reading

JEALOUSY

Jealousy is a poison that robs us of peace, contentment, and joy. It draws our minds to focus on what we do not have rather than being grateful for all we do have! Jealousy can develop into bitterness and resentment, reaping nothing but defeat and destruction. Like a fire, if it goes unchecked, will destroy goodness in our hearts and negatively impact a sound mind.

Thanksgiving is the healing salve to jealousy; it conquers the poison jealousy brings to our souls. As we practice thanksgiving, our focus is on our blessings and all the goodness the Lord brings into our lives. Let us not quench the Spirit (1 Thessalonians 5:19); but live with hearts and minds of gratitude, reaping a harvest of JOY!

PRAY!

O Lord,

Jealousy is a poison that destroys!
Take away the jealousy I feel towards

_____ *(Confess specifically)*

Fill my heart with gratitude
For you have showered me
With countless blessings!
How grateful I am for:

_____ *(Make your list)*

Thank you, thank you, Jesus!
For your plans for me
Are good, beautiful and perfect
My heart is full of praise!

Amen

✝ FROM GOD'S WORD

But godliness with contentment is great gain. For we brought nothing into this world, and it is certain we can carry nothing out.

1 TIMOTHY 6:6-7 KJV

If we are living now by the Holy Spirit's power, let us follow the Holy Spirit's leading in every part of our lives. Then we won't need to look for honors and popularity, which lead to jealously and hard feelings.

GALATIANS 5:25 TLB

In everything give thanks: for this is the will of God in Christ Jesus concerning you.

1 THESSALONIANS 5:18 KJV

💬 SPEAK IT OUT!

Jealousy will have no part in me! How grateful I am for the bounty of your blessings; as I am yours, Lord, it is all very good!

Additional Verses from Your Scripture Reading

LOVE

The greatest gift we can give others is our love. It doesn't matter whether or not it's deserved or if we are loved in return. God commands us to love one another; therefore we choose to love!

God is love. As we seek to love God first, He will develop a heart of love in us for others. As we love others without expecting love in return, we will walk in the light and our hearts will be filled with joy!

 PRAY!

Dear Lord,

As I continue to walk in the light
Please give me a heart to love others
When I hate, the darkness is within me (I John 2:10)
And makes me stumble

I choose to love others as you have commanded
In action and in truth (I John 3:18)
Most importantly, I pray I will love you
Above all, forever and always

In Jesus name,
Amen

🕇 FROM GOD'S WORD

Anyone who claims to be in the light but hates his brother is still in the darkness. Whoever loves his brother lives in the light, and there is nothing in him to make him stumble. But whoever hates his brother is in the darkness and walks around in the darkness; he does not know where he is going, because the darkness has blinded him.

I JOHN 2:9-11 NIV

My little children, let us not love in word, neither in tongue; but in deed and in truth.

I JOHN 3:18 KJV

And this is his commandment, That we should believe on the name of his Son Jesus Christ, and love one another, as he gave us commandment.

I JOHN 3:23 KJV

💬 SPEAK IT OUT!

I choose to love that I may live in the light and not stumble! (I John 2:10)

Additional Verses from Your Scripture Reading

OBEDIENCE

To know Jesus is to love him. To love him is to live for him. To live for him is to abide in him. Abiding in Christ, we desire to walk in obedience to him and strive to follow his commands. As we do, our lives become filled with peace and joy.

Our acts of obedience reflect the Holy Spirit within us and God's love is made perfect in us. Obedience enables the Lord to fulfill his purpose in our lives; and we ultimately will experience the satisfaction, joy, and blessings that result from walking with Jesus!

PRAY!

Help me, Lord, to walk daily with you
Obeying your commands and your leading
For if I don't, the truth is not in me
And I will not be perceived as one knowing you (I John 2:4)

As I walk in obedience to you, O Lord,
Your love is made complete in me (I John 2:5)
Your purpose fulfilled through me
Transform my heart to walk as Jesus did

In your precious name, Jesus,
Amen

✝ FROM GOD'S WORD

All who keep his commandments abide in him, and he in them. And by this we know that he abides in us, by the Spirit which he has given us.

1 JOHN 3:24 RSV

And by this we may be sure that we know him, if we keep his commandments. He who says "I know him" but disobeys his commandments is a liar, and the truth is not in him; but whoever keeps his word, in him truly love for God is perfected. By this we may be sure that we are in him: he who says he abides in him ought to walk in the same way in which he walked.

1 JOHN 2:3-6 RSV

I press toward the mark for the prize at the high calling of God in Christ Jesus.

PHILIPPIANS 3:14 KJV

Samuel replied, "Has the Lord as much pleasure in your burnt offerings and sacrifices as in your obedience? Obedience is far better than sacrifice. He is much more interested in your listening to him than in your offering the fat of rams to him."

1 SAMUEL 15:22 TLB

💬 SPEAK IT OUT!

I choose to obey God's commands for his truth dwells within and his love made complete in me! (I John 2:3-5)

Additional Verses from Your Scripture Reading

PEACE

God calls us to peace. If peace resides in our hearts, we can handle most anything! The peace that comes only from Jesus Christ strengthens us to walk through trials and helps us to trust. We need to surrender fear, anxiety, control, all that robs us of peace, and lay it all down at the feet of Jesus. Ask God our Father, the God of Peace, to flood your heart with his peace, the perfect peace that goes beyond our limited understanding and be thankful!

🙏 PRAY!

Fill me with your peace, O Lord,
Guarding my heart and my mind in Christ
My heart will not be troubled or afraid (John 14:27)
For the peace of Christ rules in my heart
And I am thankful! (Colossians 3:15)

Through the power of Jesus Christ
Who lives within me
I am at peace
Praise the Name of Jesus!
Amen

🔲 FROM GOD'S WORD

Let the peace of Christ rule in your hearts, since as members of one body you were called to peace. And be thankful.

COLOSSIANS 3:15 NIV

And the peace of God, which passeth all understanding, shall keep your hearts and minds through Christ Jesus.

PHILIPPIANS 4:7 KJV

Great peace have they which love thy law: and nothing shall offend them.

PSALM 119:165 KJV

Peace I leave with you, my peace I give unto you: not as the world giveth, give I unto you. Let not your heart be troubled, neither let it be afraid.

JOHN 14:27 KJV

💬 SPEAK IT OUT!

The Lord's peace is with me at all times and in every way, guarding my heart and mind in Christ Jesus!
(2 Thessalonians 3:16, Philippians 4:7)

Additional Verses from Your Scripture Reading

PEER PRESSURE

As Jesus followers, we are not to be conformed to this world or compromise Biblical truth to be accepted by others. Instead, we need to reflect the love of Jesus to all we meet by our actions and our words.

Be strong; stand firm in your faith and let nothing move you! (I Corinthians 15:58) Do not live according to the ways of an ever changing culture; rather, live God's Way, according to his Word. Don't allow your relationship with Jesus be about following a set of rules either. Instead, develop an intimate relationship with Jesus by being in his Word, in prayer with a heart of praise and thanksgiving. As we draw closer to Jesus, he transforms the heart. He alone gives us the courage to stand strong within our culture to bring him glory above all.

 PRAY!

Oh Lord, magnificent Father,
You have created me to be set apart
To reflect your love and goodness to others

Help me not to waver in my faith
In Christ, I will be strong and have courage
Resisting the enemy and the ways of the world

Help me not be conformed to the world
But be transformed by the renewing of my mind (Romans 12:2)
To live for the purpose you have for me

All for your glory!
In Jesus name,
Amen

✝ FROM GOD'S WORD

Finally, my brethren, be strong in the Lord, and in the power of his might.

EPHESIANS 6:10 KJV

The Lord is on my side; I will not fear: what can man do unto me? It is better to trust in the Lord than to put confidence in man.

PSALM 118:6, 8 KJV

And now just as you trusted Christ to save you, trust him, too, for each day's problems; live in vital union with him.

COLOSSIANS 2:6 TLB

💬 SPEAK IT OUT!

I will be strong in the Lord and in the power of his might! Transform me, Lord, by renewing my mind according to your Holy Word! (From Ephesians 6:10, Romans 12:2)

Additional Verses from Your Scripture Reading

PRIDE

Nothing good comes out of pride. It is self-seeking, self-honoring; it puffs up and will become our downfall. God is the giver of every good and perfect gift. (James 1:17) This does not mean we are to demean ourselves and not be confident. Our confidence is to be in Jesus! We need to be our best, do our best, fully aware that God is behind any "greatness" we achieve. (Psalm 18:35b) Let us therefore be God-glorifying in every aspect of our lives; our words and actions touching hearts and blessing others!

 PRAY!

Dear Lord,

I want nothing to do with sinful pride
Yet, so often pride rears its head in me
Deliver me from this stronghold
Help me to glorify you in all I think, say, and do!

May my confidence be solely in you, Lord!
Help me to strive to be my best, do my best
So that when others see me
They look to You.

In my Savior's name, Jesus, I pray,
Amen

✝ FROM GOD'S WORD

Pride goes before destruction, and a haughty spirit before a fall.

PROVERBS 16:18 RSV

A man's pride brings him low, but a man of lowly spirit gains honor.

PROVERBS 29:23 NIV

Therefore, my beloved, as you have always obeyed, so now, not only as in my presence but much more in my absence, work out your own salvation with fear and trembling; for God is at work in you, both to will and to work for his good pleasure.

PHILIPPIANS 2:12-13 RSV

💬 SPEAK IT OUT!

I cast away sinful pride; my confidence is in you, Lord, to bring you glory!

Additional Verses from Your Scripture Reading

PURPOSE

Do you believe God has a plan for your life? Does he really have a purpose specifically just for you? Or do you think your life results in consequences solely from your decisions and choices?

IF our lives are surrendered to Jesus Christ and we seek the Lord with all our hearts, he will direct our steps according to his purpose and our best. Look at what the Scriptures say. Trust and believe; his Word is truth!

 PRAY!

Dear Lord,

I don't have a clear vision as to the purpose
You have for my life
How am I to make a difference in this world?
Please direct my steps according to your will, O Lord
Show me what you've created me to accomplish

Help me develop my gifts and talents
Even my weaknesses
To prepare me for the call you have on my life
Strengthen me to do my part; lead me, Lord

You DO have a plan and a purpose for me!
Thank you that you are preparing me for good works
For my best and your glory
How I praise you, for I am yours!
In Jesus name,
Amen

✝ FROM GOD'S WORD

Being confident of this very thing, that he which hath begun a good work in you will perform it until the day of Jesus Christ:

PHILIPPIANS 1:6 KJV

For it is God which worketh in you both to will and to do of his good pleasure.

PHILIPPIANS 2:13 KJV

Many are the plans in a man's heart, but it is the Lord's purpose that prevails.

PROVERBS 19:21 NIV

💬 SPEAK IT OUT!

I praise you, Lord, for you have plans to prosper and not harm me, giving me a future and a hope! (Jeremiah 29:11)

Additional Verses from Your Scripture Reading:

REJECTION

As a child of God created in his image, you are nothing less than amazing! Living in a fallen world, rejection is inevitable. Satan will use it to defeat and destroy. We must not allow any rejection or the fear of it to hinder us from moving in the direction God has for us. Submitting to rejection leads to defeat. Take heart; be strong in the Lord and in the power of his might! (Ephesians 6:10) With Jesus, we are overcomers! (John 16:33)

Be purposeful and come against any feelings of rejection with Holy Spirit boldness! Surrender these negative, self-conscious emotions back to the Lord, and trust him. Trust him to work all things, even times of rejection, for your good as you love him and live according to his purpose. (Romans 8:38)

 PRAY!

Dear Lord,

Rejection makes me feel unloved, devalued
Yet, I am your child, created in the image of God
That makes me amazing!
Take away any fear of rejection
With your help, I will not allow it to defeat me

Flood me with your peace
Move me forward with Holy Spirit boldness,
Confident that I am in your hands!
I praise you for perfecting your will in me!
Thank you, Jesus,

Amen

🔲 FROM GOD'S WORD

So God created man in his own image, in the image of God created he him; male and female created he them.

GENESIS 1:27 KJV

So we say with confidence, "The Lord is my helper; I will not be afraid. What can man do to me?"

HEBREWS 13:6 NIV

These things I have spoken unto you, that in me ye might have peace. In the world ye shall have tribulation: but be of good cheer; I have overcome the world.

JOHN 16:33 KJV

💬 SPEAK IT OUT!

God will not reject me for I am his inheritance. (Psalm 94:14) Man's rejection has no power over me!

Additional Verses from Your Scripture Reading

STRENGTH

L ife at times makes us weary. Our work or school load is heavy, problems surmount, we experience heartache, disappointment, frustration, and difficult challenges. Our praises are being sung less and less, our thankfulness diminishes. Bodies, minds, and souls become weakened. As we cry out for strength especially through the use of God's Word, we become empowered by the Holy Spirit to face any challenge before us with victory! *God is our refuge and strength, a very present help in trouble. (Psalm 46:1 KJV)*

🙏 PRAY!

Lord Jesus,

YOU are my refuge and strength,
My ever-present help in time of need (Psalm 46:1)
I feel weak; be my strength!

Thank you for my weakness
For in my weakness your strength empowers me!
Fill me, Holy Spirit
Empower me to walk through these challenges,

_____*(State your specific challenge)*
Today with victory

You, O Lord, arm me with strength
And make my way perfect (Psalm 18:32)
I rejoice in you, Jesus!

Amen

✝ FROM GOD'S WORD

I can do all things through Christ which strengtheneth me.

PHILIPPIANS 4:13 KJV

It is God who arms me with strength and makes my way perfect.

PSALM 18:32 NIV

But he said to me, "My grace is sufficient for you, for my power is made perfect in weakness."

2 CORINTHIANS 12:9A NIV

💬 SPEAK IT OUT!

I am strong in the Lord and in his mighty power; I can do all things through Christ who strengthens me! (Ephesians 6:10, Philippians 4:13)

Additional Verses from Your Scripture Reading

THOUGHTS

Thoughts greatly impact how we live our lives. Our thought life will affect our hearts, influencing our attitudes and our actions. Let us become aware of the things we allow into our minds, those we ponder, and take captive all thoughts to the glory of Christ! (2 Corinthians 10:5)

 PRAY!

My thoughts are ugly, O Lord
I cast them away from my mind and my heart
Taking captive every thought to the glory of Christ Jesus!
(2 Corinthians 10:5)

Therefore, whatever is good
Whatever is lovely
I choose to think on these things! (Philippians 4:8)

Yes! Because of you and the power of Jesus within me
My heart is like new
My thoughts to glorify you

Praise Jesus!
Amen

✝ FROM GOD'S WORD

For to be carnally minded is death; but to be spiritually minded is life and peace.

ROMANS 8:6 KJV

For though we walk in the flesh, we do not war after the flesh: (For the weapons of our warfare are not carnal, but mighty through God to the pulling down of strong holds;) Casting down imaginations, and every high thing that exalteth itself against the knowledge of God, and bringing into captivity every thought to the obedience of Christ;

2 CORINTHIANS 10:3-5 KJV

Finally, brethren, whatsoever things are true, whatsoever things are honest, whatsoever things are just, whatsoever things are pure, whatsoever things are lovely, whatsoever things are of good report; if there be any virtue, and if there be any praise, think on these things.

PHILIPPIANS 4:8 KJV

💬 SPEAK IT OUT!

I take captive every thought to bring glory to Christ Jesus, my Lord! (2 Corinthians 10:5)

Additional Verses from Your Scripture Reading:

_____

_____

_____

VICTORY!

We are faced with countless challenges, often daily, leading either to victory or defeat. Many of these have been addressed in this book, anxiety, fear, peer pressure, to name a few. Satan's hope is to bring defeat to such a degree that it destroys. Jesus is our Victor; he alone brings us the victory!

We are given the shield of faith. We must keep it strong, trusting in God's promises to experience the victory he has for us. We are not to be carnally minded, rather, be spiritually minded. (Romans 8:6). As we allow God's Word to permeate our hearts, minds, and souls becoming our anchor for life, we become empowered to conquer ANY challenge. As we know and love Jesus, we trust him, and through the power of prayer and God's Holy Word, we will gain the victory!

🙏 PRAY!

In all things, including the things I am going through now
In this very thing, _____ *(Name your challenge)*,
I am more than a conqueror
Through Christ who loves me (Romans 8:37)
For my victory is in Jesus!

The Lord strengthens me
As I put my trust in Him
You are faithful, Lord
You deliver me from my enemies
Praise the name of Jesus!

Amen

✝ FROM GOD'S WORD

With God we will gain the victory, and he will trample down our enemies.

PSALM 60:12 NIV

In this world you will have trouble. But take heart! I have overcome the world.

JOHN 16:33B NIV

No, in all these things we are more than conquerors through him who loved us.

ROMANS 8:37 RSV

But the Lord is faithful; he will strengthen you and guard you from evil.
2 THESSALONIANS 3:3 RSV

💬 SPEAK IT OUT!

Satan has no power over me; I have victory in Jesus!
(Psalm 60:12)

Additional Verses from Your Scripture Reading

WISDOM

Wisdom comes from the Lord and out of his mouth come knowledge and understanding. (Proverbs 2:6) Pray for the desire to know him, long to be in his Word daily, and gain a heart of wisdom and discernment. The Scriptures are unchanging and do not fluctuate with the culture. Insight and understanding come from meditating upon the Scriptures and applying them to daily living.

But be doers of the word, and not hearers only, deceiving yourselves. For if any one is a hearer of the word and not a doer, he is like a man who observes his natural face in a mirror; for he observes himself and goes away and at once forgets what he was like. But he who looks into the perfect law, the law of liberty, and perseveres, being no hearer that forgets but a doer that acts, he shall be blessed in his doing.

JAMES 1:22-25 RSV

 PRAY!

O, Lord,

Give me a heart that longs for you
I want to know you better
Love you deeper
Gain wisdom and discernment
As you grow it in me.

Help me to be your faithful child
In your Word daily
For then your commands
Will be ever with me
And I will become wiser than my enemies (Psalm 119:98)

Praise you, Jesus,
Amen

✝ FROM GOD'S WORD

Do you see a man who is wise in his own eyes? There is more hope for a fool than for him.

PROVERBS 26:12 RSV

Your commands make me wiser than my enemies, for they are ever with me.

PSALM 119:98 NIV

Behold, thou desirest truth in the inward parts: and in the hidden part thou shalt make me to know wisdom.

PSALM 51:6 KJV

💬 SPEAK IT OUT!

Your commands are with me giving me a heart of wisdom and discernment! (Psalm 119:98)

Additional Verses from Your Scripture Reading

THE WORD

As we conclude this book, I hope you are acknowledging, THE POWER OF GOD'S HOLY AND MIGHTY WORD! No doubt, it is alive and active! (Hebrews 4:12) Through the indwelling of the Holy Spirit and God's Spoken Word, we have power to live in victory through all circumstances. Negative emotions and defeatist attitudes will have no power over us; instead, strength, joy and peace will abound!

I write unto you, little children, because your sins are forgiven you for his name's sake. I write unto you, fathers, because ye have known him that is from the beginning. I write unto you, young men, because ye have overcome the wicked one. I write unto you, little children, because ye have known the Father.

I JOHN 2:12-13 KJV

 PRAY!

Dear Lord,

I pray I never stop yearning daily for your Word
Enlighten me!
Speak to my heart; satisfy my soul with your love
That I might gain a heart of wisdom and discernment
And live accordingly

Because of You, I have all things:
Strength, power, love, joy, and peace
Praise your Holy Name!
Thank you for your Mighty Word
Breathing life into my soul

Amen, Dear Jesus,
Amen!

✝ FROM GOD'S WORD

I write to you, young men, because you are strong, and the word of God abides in you, and you have overcome the evil one.

1 JOHN 2:14B RSV

For the word of God is living and active. Sharper than any double-edged sword, it penetrates even to dividing soul and spirit, joints and marrow; it judges the thoughts and attitudes of the heart.

HEBREWS 4:12 NIV

All Scripture is given by inspiration of God, and is profitable for doctrine, for reproof, for correction, for instruction in righteousness:

2 TIMOTHY 3:16-17 KJV

💬 SPEAK IT OUT!

Through the power of God's Word, I have strength, peace, joy, and victory!

Additional Verses from Your Scripture Reading

BE EMPOWERED AND OVERCOME!

We are designed to be overcomers; amazing people, created in God's image to do great works for him! Be in God's Word; meditate on it daily. God's Word, his Truth, defeats the enemy! Let it saturate your heart and soul to the depths of your very being.

You will conquer daily battles in victory as you allow the power of the Holy Spirit move and work within you. The more you absorb the Scriptures, wisdom and discernment will permeate your hearts and minds. You will develop an awareness of God speaking to you and smile when you listen, obey, and experience the resulting fruit. Your life's journey will become a testimony to others; a life well lived filled with peace, joy, and victory!

Nay, in all these things we are more than conquerors through him that loved us.

ROMANS 8:37 KJV

He that overcometh shall inherit all things; and I will be his God, and he shall be my son.

REVELATION 21:7 KJV

Now it's your turn
Use these pages to create your own prayers

While reading your Bible, write down verses that speak to your heart and use them to create your own prayers. As you journal and develop personal prayers through God's Word, commit them to memory; they will be with you wherever you go for whatever you need. You will be praying in God's language, and your heart and soul will be blessed!

Once you experience victory that comes through the power of praying and speaking out the Scriptures, I would love to hear from you! Please email me with your thoughts at:

cherdela7@gmail.com

and share your experiences with me. How exciting it will be to hear your testimonies as you live daily through the power of God's Spoken Word onto victory!

The Lord be with you now and forevermore,
CHERYL

SPEAK IT OUT!

Bibliography

The Holy Bible
King James Version by Public Domain

Life Application Study Bible, *New International Version*
Wheaton: Zondervan Publishing House, 2005

New American Standard Bible *(NASB)*
Bible Gateway. Web. 30 Oct. 2017
Copyright © 1960, 1962, 1963, 1968, 1971, 1972, 1973, 1975, 1977, 1995 by The Lockman Foundation

The Guideposts Parallel Bible
Grand Rapids: Zondervan Corporation, 1973
Living Bible Wheaton: Tyndale House Publishers, 1971
Revised Standard Version, Zondervan Publishing House, Licensee, 1971 by Division of Christian Education of the National Council of Churches of Christ in the United States of America.

CPSIA information can be obtained
at www.ICGtesting.com
Printed in the USA
FFOW03n2255150318
45696464-46533FF